Contents

7 p60	In the playground	*There is / There are* Prepositions: in, on, under, next to *Let's (go to the park).*	R: My town L: Identify location. S: Decide what to do.	L: Identify location. W: *and* and *but*. Write about your town.
8 p66	Hobbies	*can*: affirmative, negative, questions and short answers	R: story *Where's my mobile phone?*	L: Identify the correct answer. W: Commas with *and* in a list. Write about your bedroom.
Science p72 Our senses		*We smell with our noses. We can smell flowers and plants.*	Project: Write about your senses.	
Review 4 p74		Phonics: /eɪ/		
9 p76	Food	present simple: *like, want* affirmative, negative, questions and short answers	R: What's on the menu? L: Identify likes and dislikes S: Order food and drink	L: Identify what children like and don't like. W: *and, or* and *but*. Write about what you like and don't like.
10 p82	Daily routines	present simple for routines *at (seven) o'clock, every day, on (Monday)*	R: story *Superboy!*	L: Identify the correct information. W: Identify verbs. Write about what you do after school.
Social Science p88 A healthy life		Healthy Harry (eats fruit every day).	Project: Write about your life.	
Review 5 p90		Phonics: /aɪ/		
11 p92	Activities, Clothes	present continuous: affirmative	R: Me and my friends L: Identify the children. S: Describe and identify the correct child.	L: Identify the correct information. W: Short forms of *is* and *has*. Write you and a friend.
12 p98	Sports	present continuous: negative, questions and short answers	R: story *Jane and the giant*	L: Identify the correct activity. W: Apostrophes. Write about what you, your family and friends are doing.
Social Science p104 Other homes		*My home is (a flat). There are (two bedrooms).*	Project: Compare your homes.	
Review 6 p106		Phonics: /əʊ/		

The Yazoo Music Show p108

World Animal Day p110

International Children's Day p112

Alphabet Aa–Zz

 Listen, point and say.

 Listen and chant.

Aa

apple

Bb

bear

Cc

cat

Dd

dog

Ee

elephant

Kk

kangaroo

Ll

lion

Mm

monkey

Nn

nest

Ss

snake

Tt

tiger

Uu

umbrella

Vv

violin

Ff

flower

Gg

goat

Hh

hippo

Ii

insect

Jj

jelly

Oo

octopus

Pp

penguin

Qq

queen

Rr

rabbit

Ww

whale

Xx

fo**x**

Yy

yo-yo

Zz

zebra

Numbers 1-20

1 Listen, point and say. •))

1 one

2 two

3 three

4 four

5 five

6 six

7 seven

8 eight

9 nine

10 ten

11 eleven

12 twelve

13 thirteen

14 fourteen

15 fifteen

16 sixteen

17 seventeen

18 eighteen

19 nineteen

20 twenty

2 Look at 1. Listen and circle. •))

3 Sing along with the band! •))

One, two, three, four, five.
Count from one to twenty!
Six, seven, eight, nine, ten.
Count from one to twenty!
Eleven, twelve, thirteen,
Fourteen, fifteen.
Count from one to twenty!
Sixteen, seventeen,
Eighteen, nineteen, twenty.
Count from one to twenty!

4 Find, count and write.

___three___ goats   _____ snakes   _____ monkeys   _____ nests

_____ rabbits   _____ apples   _____ insects   _____ flowers

5 Ask and answer.

How many goats?   Three.

Right. Your turn.

6 Play the game.

Colours

1 Listen, point and say. •))

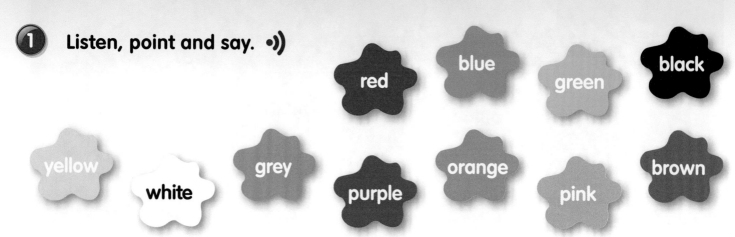

red   blue   green   black

yellow   white   grey   purple   orange   pink   brown

2 Look and circle.

What colour is it?

1 green / (blue)

2 pink / grey

3 purple / brown

4 black / yellow

5 white / red

6 orange / blue

7 yellow / white

8 black / grey

3 Sing along with the band! •))

Red and white and pink,
Yellow, green and blue.
Grey and black and brown,
Orange and purple too.
Colours in the zoo for you!

4 Listen and number. •))

 □

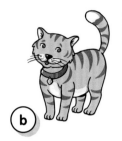 □

 1

 □

a   b   c   d

5 Write. Then play the game.

red _____ _____ _____

_____ _____ _____ _____

_____ _____ _____

What colour is it?

It's a fox.

It's orange.

Yes.

It's a school!

1 Listen, point and say. •))

 school   desk   bag   pencil case   pen   rubber   notebook

2 Listen and read. •))

3 Read and circle.

1 It's a desk.
yes / no

2 It's a pencil.
yes / no

3 It's a rubber. /
yes / no

4 It's a bag.
yes / no

4 Let's learn! Listen and say. •))

What's this? — It's a notebook.

What's this? — It's an umbrella.

5 Listen and stick. Then circle. •))

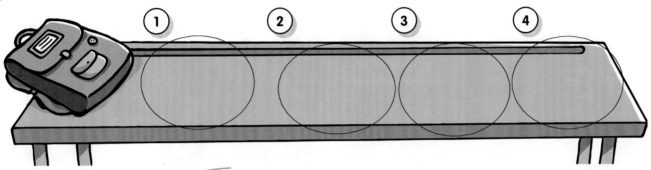

1 What's this? It's a (notebook) / rubber.
2 What's this? It's a rubber / pencil case.

3 What's this? It's a notebook / pen.
4 What's this? It's an apple / umbrella.

6 Write a or an.

1 It's __a__ bag.
2 It's _____ octopus.

3 It's _____ elephant.
4 It's _____ desk.

7 Sing along with the band! •))

What's this? What is this?
What's this in my bag?
What's this? What is this?
What's this in my bag?
What's this? It's a pencil.
A pencil and a pen.
A pencil, a rubber, a book and a pen.
A pencil, a rubber, a book and a pen.

13

1b Spell 'octopus'.

1 Listen, point and say. 🔊

 ruler   chair   board   spell   write   clean   be quiet

2 Listen and read. 🔊

1
What's this?
It's a chair.
Yes. Spell 'chair', please.
c...h...a...i...r

2
Very good, Patty! Tag, write on the board, please. Write 'ruler'.
ruler
Thank you, Tag. Clean the board, please.

3
Karla, what's this?
It's an octopus. It's purple.
I'm an octopus.

4
Be quiet, please, Chatter.
Spell 'octopus'!
o...k...a...
No. It's o...c...t...

3 Read again and match.

1 Spell   a   quiet , please.
2 Write on   b   'ruler', please.
3 Be   c   the board, please.

4 Let's learn! Listen and say. •))

What's this?
What colour is it?

It's an octopus.
It's purple.

5 Read and match.

1 It's a bag.   **2** It's a notebook.   **3** It's an umbrella.   **4** It's a pencil case.

It's yellow.   It's pink and blue.   It's red.   It's orange and purple.

6 Look at 5. Point, ask and answer.

What's this?   It's a bag.
What colour is it?   It's pink and blue.

7 Play the game.

Spell 'apple', please.

a...p...p...l...e.

Very good!

My classroom

1 **What can you see in the classroom? Point and say.**

board   ruler   notebook   desk   bag   cat   chair   pencil case

2 **Listen and read. Then number.** •))

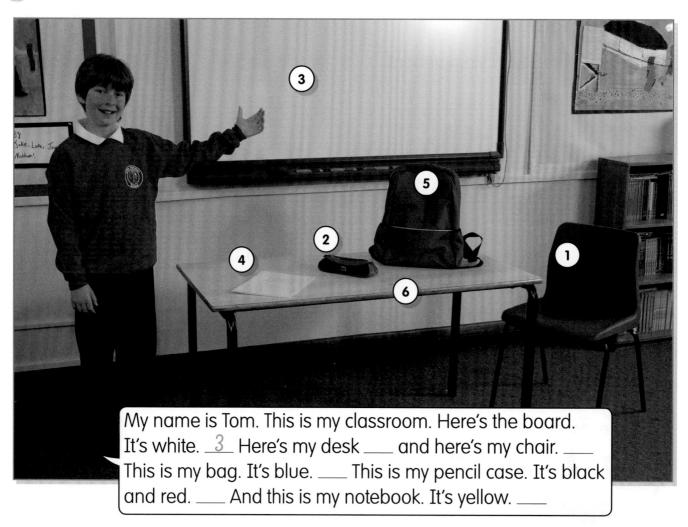

My name is Tom. This is my classroom. Here's the board. It's white. _3_ Here's my desk ___ and here's my chair. ___ This is my bag. It's blue. ___ This is my pencil case. It's black and red. ___ And this is my notebook. It's yellow. ___

3 **Read again and match.**

1 It's blue. _c_
2 It's white. _____
3 It's yellow. _____
4 It's black and red. _____

4 Listen and circle. •))

1

A   B   C

2

A   B   C

3

A   B   C

5 Look at 4 and write A, B or C.

1 It's green. ___A___

2 It's a ruler. _____

3 Write 'chair' on the board, please. _____

6 Play the game. page 99

What colour is your bag?

It's black and red.

Cars and dolls

1 **Listen, point and say.** •))

 balloon   car   doll   stickers   crayon   card

2 **Listen and read.** •))

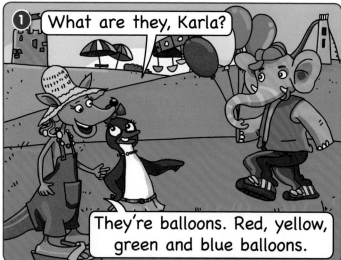

1 What are they, Karla?

They're balloons. Red, yellow, green and blue balloons.

2 What are they?

They're cars. Orange cars.

Trumpet! Come here, please.

3 What are they, Sally?

They're dolls and stickers and crayons.

4 Look! A card!

Happy Birthday Sally

3 **Read and tick or cross.**

1 green balloons ✓ **2** black cars ___ **3** yellow stickers ___ **4** blue crayons ___

4 Let's learn! Listen and say. •))

What are they?

How many balls?

They're balls.

One ball, two balls, three balls.

5 Look and circle. Then say how many.

1 balloon / balloons   **2** doll / dolls   **3** car / cars   **4** crayon / crayons

6 Ask and answer.

Number five. What are they?

They're crayons.

How many crayons?

Five.

What colour are they?

Green.

1    2    3

4   5    6

7   8   9

7 Sing along with the band! •))

Orange cars and
Yellow cars.
Cars for me and you!
One, two, three, four.
Lots of cars.
Cars for me and you.

Purple dolls and
Big, pink dolls.
Dolls for me and you!
One, two, three, four.
Lots of dolls.
Dolls for me and you.

That's a robot!

1 Listen, point and say. •))

 cake
 birthday
 present
 watch
 robot

2 Listen and read. •))

It's my birthday. This is my cake.
Happy Birthday, Sally!
Thank you.

What are they?
They're your presents.

This is a watch and that's a pen.
Thank you. They're lovely presents.

That's a robot.
Thank you, Tag!

3 Read again. Find and circle the name.

1 This is my cake. Sally / Karla
2 They're your presents. Chatter / Patty

3 This is a watch. Patty / Tag
4 Thank you, Tag. Tag / Sally

4 **Let's learn!** Listen and say. •))

5 Listen and stick. Then circle. •))

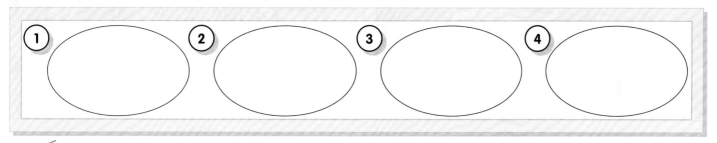

1 (This is) / That's a robot.   **3** This is / That's a balloon.
2 This is / That's a car.   **4** This is / That's a watch.

6 Look at 5. Point, ask and answer.

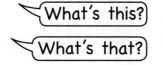

What's this?   This is a ...
What's that?   That's a ...

7 Play the game.

The frogs!

1 What's this? It's a school. Look! A teacher.

2 Look! What are they? Frogs!

3 Lots of frogs!

Close the door!

4 Close the window!

1 Listen, point and say. •))

2 Listen and read. •))

3 Look and match.

 a

 b

 c

 d

1 Open the door. **2** Close the window. **3** Sit down. **4** Stand up.

teacher
 door
 window
 close
 open
 stand up
 sit down

4 **Count and write.**

1 _four frogs_   2 _____   3 _____

5 **Listen again. Then act out.** •))

23

Social Science

I'm Helen. I'm in year 2. This is my school.

1 Listen, point and read. •))

This is the office. You can see Mrs White, the secretary.

This is the hall. That's Mr Barnes. He's the head teacher.

Look! This is my classroom. Here's Mrs Norman. She's my teacher. She's nice.

Can you see the pupils in the library? They're very quiet!

Here's the canteen. That's Mrs Butler. She's the cook.

2 Listen and number. •))

3 Read again and circle.

1 Number 1 is the hall / canteen.
2 Number 2 is the office / classroom.
3 Number 3 is the library / canteen.

4 Number 4 is the office / hall.
5 Number 5 is the classroom / library.

4 Listen and number. •))

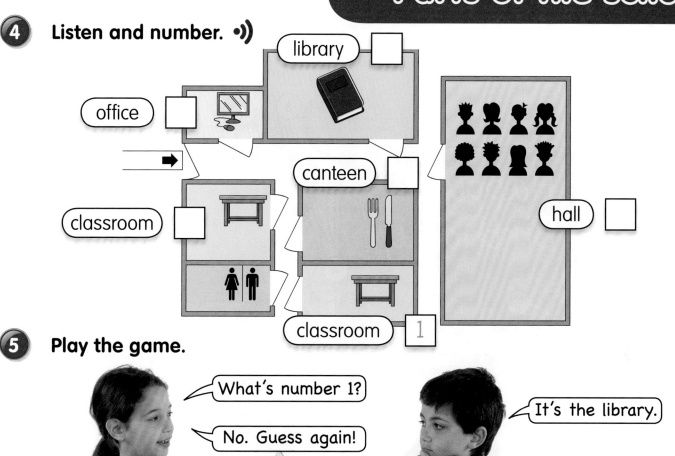

library ☐

office ☐

canteen ☐

classroom ☐

hall ☐

classroom 1

5 Play the game.

What's number 1?

No. Guess again!

It's the library.

6 Your project! Write about your school. Draw a picture.

My school
This is the canteen.
That's the cook.
They're pupils.

Greg Class 2b

Review 1

1 Look and number.

board	2
desk	
notebook	
ruler	
cards	
balloons	
cake	
presents	
watch	
stickers	

2 Look at 1. Point, ask and answer.

What's that?   It's a board.

What are they?   They're stickers.

3 Listen and do.

4 Listen and chant.

Ten red pens in Tag's black bag.

5 **Do the quiz.**

① This is _____ octopus.

② How many balls?

③ This is a _____.

④ What's that?

⑤ Count to twenty.

⑥ Say the colours.

⑦ What's this?

⑧ How many pencils?

⑨ What are they?

⑩ What colour is it?

⑪ They're _____ and _____ apples.

⑫ What's this?

⑬ This is a _____.

START

FINISH

WELL DONE!

3a

She's pretty.

1 Listen, point and say. 🔊

sunny

family

mum

dad

brother

sister

2 Listen and read. 🔊

1 It's sunny.

Hello, Patty!

Hello! Meet my family. This is my mum and dad.

2 He's Peter. He's my brother.

Hello. I'm Trumpet.

I'm Chatter.

Hello.

3 Who's she?

She's my sister, Peggy.

She's pretty.

4 Help!

Sorry, Chatter.

3 Find and circle. Then say.

1 Sister.

2

3

4

4 Let's learn! Listen and say. •))

I'm Trumpet. I'm an elephant.

You're Patty.

He's Peter.   She's Peggy.

5 Listen and stick. Then circle. •))

1 She's my mum /(sister).
2 He's my dad / brother.

3 He's my dad / brother.
4 She's my mum / sister.

6 Look at 5. Point, ask and answer.

Who's she?

She's my ...

7 Sing along with the band! •))

Clap and dance and sing with me.
Sing about my family.
He's my brother.
She's my sister.
He's my dad
And she's my mum.
Clap and dance and sing with me.
Sing about my family.

Is he your grandpa?

1 Listen, point and say. •))

 baby

 boy

 girl

 grandma

grandpa

 friend

2 Listen and read. •))

1 A baby. Are you a boy?
No, I'm not. I'm a girl.
She's my sister.

2 Is she your grandma?
Yes, she is.

3 Is he your grandpa?
No, he isn't. He's my friend. He's nice!

4 He's my grandpa!

3 Find and circle. Then say.

1 She's my sister.   2   3   4

4 Let's learn! Listen and say. •))

Are you a boy?

Are you a girl?

No, I'm not.

Yes, I am.

Is he your brother?

Is he your friend?

No, he isn't.

Yes, he is.

5 Listen and circle. •))

1 Yes, she is. /
No, she isn't.

2 Yes, he is. /
No, he isn't.

3 Yes, he is. /
No, he isn't.

4 Yes, it is. /
No, it isn't.

6 Point, ask and answer.

1 ... a teacher? **2** ... a boy? **3** ... a baby? **4** ... a robot?

Is she a teacher?

No, she isn't. She's a girl.

7 Make cards. Then play the game.

page 101

Are you a
monkey?

Are you a
kangaroo?

No, I'm not.

Yes, I am.
Here you are.

31

My family

1 Who can you see in each photo? Point and say.

mum   dad   grandma   grandpa   boy   girl   baby

2 Listen and read. Then match. •))

a

b

1

c

1

Hello. I'm Polly. I'm nine.
Sam is my brother.
He's twelve. He's nice.
Lucy is my sister
and she's six.

2

Hi! I'm Will and
I'm nine.
This is my family –
mum, dad, my sister
Vicky, grandpa and me.
Grandpa is funny!

3

I'm a girl.
My name is Sarah
and I'm six.
This is my family.
Look at my baby sister,
Daisy. She's pretty.

3 Read again. Write Yes, he / she is or No, he / she isn't.

1 Is Polly ten?   No, she isn't.
2 Is Sam nice?   _____
3 Is Will eleven?   _____
4 Is Grandpa funny?   _____
5 Is Sarah eight?   _____
6 Is Daisy a baby?   _____

4 Listen and number. 🔊

a

b

c

d 1

e

f

5 Look at 4. Choose and write.

mum   ~~dad~~   grandma   grandpa   brother   friend

1 He's my ___dad___.
2 She's my _____.
3 She's my _____.

4 He's my _____.
5 She's my _____.
6 He's my _____.

6 Draw. Then ask and answer.

Who's he?

Is he funny?

He's my grandpa, James.

Yes, he is.

We're cowboys.

1 Listen, point and say. •))

box   clothes   spy   dancer   cowboy

2 Listen and read. •))

1 Wow! Look!
Let's go.

2 Open the box. What are they?
They're clothes.

3 Wow, Patty! You're a spy.
You're a dancer.

4 We're cowboys! Be careful, Chatter.
Sorry, Trumpet.

3 Read again and circle.

1 Is Patty a spy?   Yes, she is. / No, she isn't.
2 Is Karla a cowboy?   Yes, she is. / No, she isn't.
3 Is Chatter a dancer?   Yes, he is. / No, he isn't.

4 Let's learn! Listen and say. •))

5 Read and circle.

1 We're dancers.

a   b

2 You're cowboys.

a   b

3 They're girls.

a   b

4 They're clothes.

a   b

6 Look at 5. Point, ask and answer.

What are they?   They're dancers.

7 Sing along with the band! •))

Stand up and say
We're happy today,
Happy today, happy today.

Sit down and say
We're happy today,
Happy today, happy today.

Clap hands and say
We're happy today,
Happy today,
happy today.

4b Are we pirates?

1 Listen, point and say. •))

 pirate

 clown

 king

 crown

2 Listen and sing. •))

1 Are we pirates?
Are we clowns?
Are we kings
With golden crowns?
Look and see,
Look and see,
What are we?
Look and see,
Look and see,
What are we?

2 Are we dancers?
Are we clowns?
Are we queens
With golden crowns?
Look and see,
Look and see,
What are we?
Look and see,
Look and see,
What are we?

3 Are they dancers?
Are they clowns?
Are they queens
With golden crowns?
Look and say,
Look and say,
What are they?
Look and say,
Look and say,
What are they?

4 Are they pirates?
Are they clowns?
Are they kings
With golden crowns?
Look and say,
Look and say,
What are they?
Look and say,
Look and say,
What are they?

3 Look at 2 and circle.

1 Tag is a cowboy / (pirate).
2 Chatter isn't a pirate / king.
3 Karla is a spy / clown.
4 Patty isn't a clown / queen.

4. Let's learn! Listen and say. •))

5. Listen and circle. •))

1 Yes, we are. /
~~No, we aren't.~~ (circled)

2 Yes, they are. /
No, they aren't.

3 Yes, we are. /
No, we aren't.

4 Yes, they are. /
No, they aren't.

6. Point, ask and answer.

1 Are they clowns?

2 Are they queens?

3 Are they crowns?

4 Are they cowboys?

5 Are they pirates?

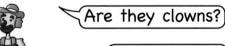

Are they clowns?

Yes, they are.

7. Make cards. Then play the game. page 103

Are they clowns?

No, they aren't.

Are they kings?

Yes, they are. Here you are.

The grey duck

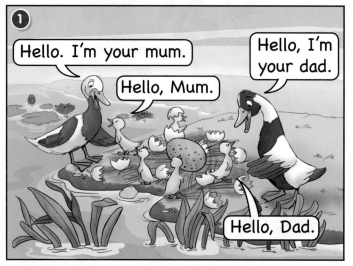

1 Listen, point and say. •))

2 Listen and read. •))

3 Look and match.

 a

 b

 c

 d

1 She's a swan.   **2** They're ducks.   **3** He's big.   **4** They're happy.

duck   swan   sad   happy   small   big

5

Is he my brother?

No, he isn't. He's small and you're big.

6

The grey duck is sad.

Goodbye!

Bye, bye.

7

Hello, my baby. I'm your mum.

Am I a swan?

Yes, you are! We're swans.

8

I love you.

I love you, Mum.

They are a happy family.

4 **Look and circle.**

1 Is she small?
(Yes, she is.) / No, she isn't.

2 Is she a swan?
Yes, she is. / No, she isn't.

3 Is he sad?
Yes, he is. / No, he isn't.

4 Are they a family?
Yes, they are. /
No, they aren't.

5 **Listen again. Then act out.** •))

39

Can you count to a hundred?

1 Listen, point and read. Then match. •))

I'm Mrs Jones. I'm a Maths teacher. Do you like Maths? Can you count to 100? Can you count to 100 in English? Look, it's easy.

50	ten
30	twenty
40	thirty
10	forty
70	fifty
20	sixty
80	seventy
100	eighty
60	ninety
90	a hundred

2 Write the numbers. Then say.

10   20   30   40   ___   60   ___   80   ___   100

3 Add. Then ask and answer.

+	10	20	30	40	50
10	20	30	40	___	___
20	30	40	___	60	___
30	___	50	60	___	___
40	50	___	___	80	___
50	60	70	80	___	100

Thirty and thirty.

Sixty!

Right. Your turn.

4 **Match. Then listen and say.** •))

Numbers 20 to 29 are easy, too! Look!

20	twenty-six
21	twenty-two
22	twenty-seven
23	twenty-four
24	twenty-five
25	twenty
26	twenty-three
27	twenty-nine
28	twenty-one
29	twenty-eight

5 **Write the numbers. Then say.**

Thirty and one is thirty-one.

31 → 30 + __1__
33 → 30 + _____
35 → 30 + _____
39 → 30 + _____

6 **Listen and circle.** •))

1 (forty-two) / twenty-four
2 fifty-five / fifty-four
3 sixty-six / sixty-seven

4 thirty-seven / seventy-three
5 eighty-one / eighty-nine
6 forty-nine / ninety-four

7 **Your project!** Make a number square. Then ask and answer.

Ninety and eight.

Ninety-eight.

Right. Your turn.

0	1	2	3	4	5	6	7	8	9
10	11	12	13	14	15	16	17	18	19
20	21	22	23	24	25	26	27	28	29
30	31	32	33	34	35	36	37	38	39
40	41	42	43	44	45	46	47	48	49
50	51	52	53	54	55	56	57	58	59
60	61	62	63	64	65	66	67	68	69
70	71	72	73	74	75	76	77	78	79
80	81	82	83	84	85	86	87	88	89
90	91	92	93	94	95	96	97	98	99

Review 2

1 **Listen and number.** •))

a ☐ b ☐ c ☐ d ☐ e 1 f ☐ g ☐

2 **Look at 1 and write.**

grandma   friends   mum   ~~dad~~   brother   grandpa   sister
cowboy   dancers   spy   queen   clown   pirate   king

1 He's my ___dad___ .   He's a _____ .
2 She's my _____ .   She's a _____ .
3 He's my _____ .   He's a _____ .
4 She's my _____ .   She's a _____ .
5 He's my _____ .   He's a _____ .
6 She's my _____ .   She's a _____ .
7 They're my _____ .   They're _____ .

3 **Look at 1. Point, ask and answer.**

> Is dad a cowboy?   No, he isn't.
> Is he a spy?   Yes, he is.

4 **Listen and chant.** •))

♪ Six big kings with ten red desks. ♪

5 Do the trail.

It's his kite.

1 Listen, point and say. ·))

 cloudy   kite   computer game   radio   bike   old   new

2 Listen and read. ·))

3 Read again. Find and circle the name.

1 It's my computer game. (Karla) / Chatter
2 It's my new bike. Tag / Chatter

3 It's my radio. Sally / Karla
4 It's my kite. Chatter / Tag

4 **Let's learn!** Listen and say. •))

This is his kite.   This is her doll.   Its clothes are pink.

5 **Listen and stick. Then circle.** •))

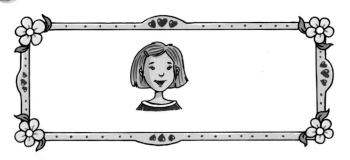 

1 (His)/ Her bike is blue.   4 His / Her car is green.
2 His / Her ball is orange.   5 His / Her book is yellow.
3 His / Her radio is red.   6 His / Her kite is pink.

6 **Read and write** his, her **or** its.

1 That's Karla. That's ____her____ computer game.
2 That's Rob and that's _____ sister. _____ name is Vicky.
3 That's my rabbit. _____ name is Fluff.

7 **Sing along with the band!** •))

What's this? What's that?   What's this? What's that?
What's this? What's that?   What's this? What's that?
What's this? What's that?   What's this? What's that?
What a terrible mess!   What a terrible mess!
This is her radio.   That is his bike.
This is her radio.   That is his bike.
This is her radio.   That is his bike.
Her radio is blue.   His bike is new.

5b — They're our toys.

1 Listen, point and say. •))

 toys
 rollerblades
 train
 winner
 prize
 fast
 slow

2 Listen and read. •))

1
I've got lots of toys.
They're **our** toys, Chatter.

2
What are they?
They're my rollerblades.
They're cool.

3
Here are Patty and Trumpet. Wow! Look at their train.
They're slow. I'm fast.
Let's race!

4
We're the winners!
Here are your prizes.
Thank you, Sally.

3 Read again and circle.

1 It's his bike.
~~yes~~ / no

2 It's her train.
yes / no

3 They're the winners.
yes / no

46

4 Let's learn! Listen and say. •))

Our bikes are old.

Their train is fast.

Your prizes are here.

5 Look and circle.

1. They're your / our birthday presents.

2. Here's your / their kite.

3. Look at their / our dog.

4. This is their / our new car.

6 Choose and write.

Her   my   your   His   ~~My~~   Their   My   your

Hi. ___My___ name is Jane.
What's _____ name?

Hi. _____ name is Anna. This is my brother. _____ name is David.

And they're _____ friends.
_____ names are Tom and Fred.

Is that _____ mum?

No, she's our teacher. _____ name is Mrs Brown.

7 Listen and check. Then act out. •))

5c Our favourite toys.

1 What toys can you see? Point and say.

2 Listen and read. Then match. •))

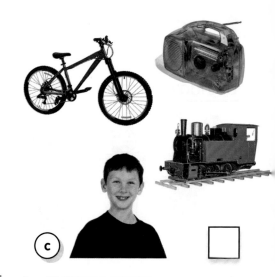

(a) ☐   (b) 1   (c) ☐

1

Here are my toys.
This is *my* computer game.
This is *my* ball. It's brown.
My favourite toy is *my*
doll. Its clothes are pink.

2

Here are my toys.
This is my radio.
It's blue.
This is my train.
It's red and green.
My favourite toy is
my bike. It's purple.

3

Here are my toys.
This is my car. It's red.
They're my rollerblades.
They're grey.
My favourite toy is my
kite. It's yellow.

3 Read again and write.

1 _____His_____ favourite toy is _____ . It's _yellow_ .

2 _____ favourite toy is _____ . Its clothes are _____ .

3 _____ favourite toy is _____ . It's _____ .

4 Listen and match. •))

1 Anna
2 Ben
3 Sue
4 Tony

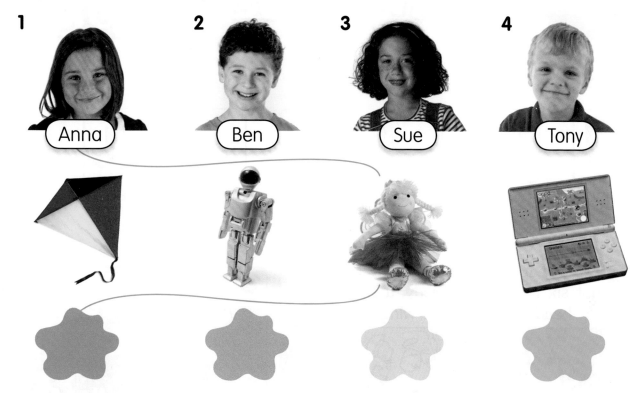

5 Look at 4 and write the names.

1 His favourite toy is a robot.   _Tony_
2 Her favourite colour is pink.   _____
3 Their favourite toy is a doll.   _____ and _____
4 Their favourite colour is green.   _____ and _____

6 Ask, answer and write.

What's your favourite toy?

It's a ....

What's your favourite colour?

It's ....

7 Tell the class.

Adam. His favourite toy is a robot.

Kim and Fred. Their favourite colour is red.

6a She's got a pet.

1 Listen, point and say.

 head
 body
 arm
 leg
 hand
 feet
 wing

2 Listen and read.

1 I've got a pet. It's an insect. It's got six legs, a blue body, a small head and beautiful wings.

2 She's got a pet. She's lucky. I haven't got a pet.
Let's look at the insects.

3 They've got lots of legs.
Look. That's big.

4 They're on my hands and arms!
They're on my feet!
Oh, dear!

3 Read again and write.

1 Its body is ___blue___.
2 Its head is _____.
3 Its wings are _____.
4 It's her _____.

4 Let's learn! Listen and say. •))

She's got a pet.

It's got six legs.

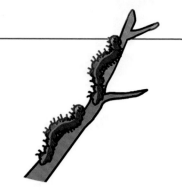
They've got lots of legs.

5 Look and match.

a

b

c

d

e

f

1 He's got a big head. ___b___
2 She's got small hands. _____
3 It's got a yellow and black body. _____

4 They've got wings. _____
5 It's got big feet. _____
6 They've got long legs. _____

6 Look at 5 and say.

It's got big feet.

c, the rabbit

7 Sing along with the band! •))

We are boys and we are girls.
We've got hands and we've got feet.
We've got arms and we've got legs.
Let's all dance now to the beat.

Clap your hands and turn around.
Stamp your feet and touch the ground.
Clap your hands and turn around.
Stamp your feet and then sit down.

6b Has it got wings?

1 Listen, point and say. •))

 ear

 mouth

 nose

 eye

 butterfly

 hair

 hair slide

2 Listen and read. •))

1. They're everywhere. Quick!
My ears.
My mouth.
My nose. Atishoo!

3. It's a present for you, Chatter.
Thank you! Now I've got a pet.
Oh, look! You've got a butterfly in your hair, Sally.

2. Have we got all the insects?
No, we haven't. Look.
Wow! It's got beautiful eyes. Has it got wings?
Yes, it has.

4. No, I haven't. Look. It's a hair slide!

3 Read again and write yes or no.

1 Sally has got a present for Tag. __no__
2 Chatter has got a pet. _____
3 His insect has got beautiful eyes. _____
4 Sally has got a butterfly. _____

52

4 Let's learn! Listen and say. •))

  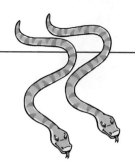

Has Chatter got a pet?
Yes, he has.

Has it got hands?
No, it hasn't.

Have they got wings?
No, they haven't.

5 Listen and circle. •))

1 ⓐ  ⓑ    2 ⓐ  ⓑ

3 ⓐ  ⓑ

6 Read and write Yes, they have **or** No, they haven't.

1 Have elephants got big ears? ___Yes, they have.___
2 Have snakes got hair? _____
3 Have swans got wings? _____
4 Have zebras got arms? _____

7 Make cards. Then play the game. page 105

Has it got four legs?   No, it hasn't.
Has it got wings?   Yes, it has.
Is it a butterfly?   Yes, it is.
Here you are.

6c Sam, the circus boy!

Look at the clowns. They're very funny. They've got long arms and legs. I've got short arms and legs. I'm not funny.

Look at the dancers. They're very beautiful. They've got beautiful feet and hands. I'm not beautiful.

Look at the monkeys. They're very fast. I'm not fast.

1 Listen, point and say. •))

2 Listen and read. •))

3 Read again and circle.

1 The clowns are (funny) / strong.
2 The dancers are beautiful / funny.
3 The monkeys are slow / fast.

4 The elephants are strong / slow.
5 Their trunks are big / small.
6 Sam is a girl / a star.

circus	star	trunk	funny	long	short	strong

Look at the elephants. They're strong. They've got big trunks. I'm not very strong.

A small boy! Have we got a small boy in the circus?

Yes, we have!

Hooray! You're a star!

4 **Read again and circle.**

1 Have the clowns got long arms and legs?   Yes, they have. / No, they haven't.
2 Has Sam got long arms and legs?   Yes, he has. / No, he hasn't.
3 Have the dancers got beautiful hands?   Yes, they have. / No, they haven't.
4 Have the elephants got small trunks?   Yes, they have. / No, they haven't.
5 Have they got a small boy in the circus?   Yes, they have. / No, they haven't.

5 **Listen again. Then act out.** •))

Science

Have kangaroos got fur?

1 **Listen, point and read.** •))

a

This is a kangaroo. Kangaroos have got big legs and short arms. They've got long tails. They've got brown fur. Some kangaroos have got grey fur.

b

1

This is a whale. Whales have got very big bodies and strong tails. They haven't got arms or legs.

c

This is a snake. Snakes have got scales on their bodies. They've got small heads. They haven't got arms or legs but they've got tails.

d

This is a penguin. Penguins have got black and white feathers. They've got short legs and big feet. They haven't got arms but they've got wings. They've got tails, too.

2 **Listen and number.** •))

3 **Read again and circle.**

1 Kangaroos have got fur. yes / no
2 Kangaroos have got scales. yes / no
3 Whales have got arms. yes / no
4 Whales have got big bodies. yes / no

5 Snakes have got scales. yes / no
6 Snakes have got tails. yes / no
7 Penguins have got feathers. yes / no
8 Penguins have got legs. yes / no

4 **Look and tick or cross.**

	feathers	legs	fur	wings	tail
	✗	✔			

5 **Ask and answer.**

Say four animals with tails.

Kangaroo, tiger, rabbit, snake.

Right!

6 **Your project!** Write about your favourite animal. Find a picture.

Elephants are my favourite animals.
They've got big bodies.
They've got long legs and tails.
They haven't got fur.

Review 3

1 **Find and write.**

kite ~~bike~~ doll car rabbit rollerblades dog hair slide radio

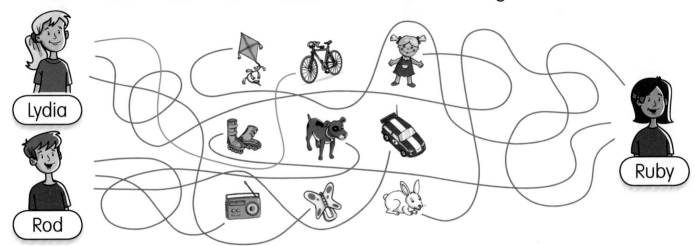

1 Lydia has got a _____ bike _____ , a _____ and a _____ .
2 Rod has got a _____ , a _____ and a _____ .
3 Ruby has got a _____ , _____ and a _____ .

2 **Look at 1. Ask and answer.**   Has Lydia got a bike?   Yes, she has.

3 **Listen and circle.** •))

1 (a)   (b)   **2** (a)  (b)

3 (a)   (b)   **4** (a)   (b)

4 **Listen and chant.** •))

  Lots of frogs have fun in the sun.

5 **Do the quiz.**

START

1 He's got short _____ .

2 Has he got a new computer game?

3 Have whales got fur?

4 The rollerblades are _____ .

5 Has it got a big nose?

6 Their bikes are _____ .

7 Its _____ are green.

8 Have penguins got black and white feathers?

9 This is our favourite _____ .

10 Has the king got a crown?

11 This is his _____ .

12 Has she got a small mouth?

13 Have they got long legs?

WELL DONE!

FINISH

59

There's a town.

1 **Listen, point and say.** •))

 tree

 house

 swimming pool

 park

 river

 playground

children

2 **Listen and read.** •))

Karla and Patty are in the treehouse.

It's fantastic here! Look! There's a town.

I can see a big house and a swimming pool.

There's a park and a river. The trees and flowers are very pretty.

Look at the playground. There are lots of children here today.

Look! Chatter is with the children.

Let's go to the playground.

3 **Look at 2. Find and number.**

the town ___1___   the swimming pool _____   the children _____
the river _____   the park _____   the playground _____

4 Let's learn! Listen and say. •))

There's a tiger in the zoo.
There are lots of animals too.
There are giraffes and hippos.

5 Listen and stick. Then write. •))

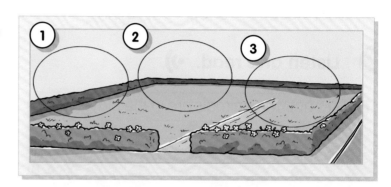

1 There are _____two trees_____ .
2 There's a _____ .
3 There's a _____ .

6 Look and say.

There are four trees.   Picture a.

7 Sing along with the band! •))

There are lots of animals in our zoo.
Lions, tigers and kangaroos.
Bears and monkeys and zebras too.
We love the animals and they love you.

There are lots of animals in our zoo.
Snakes, penguins and cockatoos.
Goats and hippos and elephants too.
We love the animals and they love you.

1 Listen, point and say. •))

 treehouse
 shop
 swing
 slide
 climbing frame
 bus
 hot

2 Listen and read. •))

1 It's hot. The animals are in the playground.

Where's Chatter?

I don't know. He isn't in the treehouse and he isn't in the shop.

2 He isn't on the swing.

He isn't under the slide.

He isn't on the climbing frame.

3 Look. There's Chatter. He's next to the bus.

4 Chatter, come here, please.

Sorry, Sally. Goodbye.

Goodbye, Chatter.

3 Look at 2 and circle.

1 There's a green climbing frame. (yes)/ no
2 There are two swings. yes / no
3 There's a yellow bus. yes / no
4 There are six children. yes / no

62

4 Let's learn! Listen and say. •))

Where's Tag? He's in the bag.
Where are Tag and Chatter?
They're next to the bag.

1   2   3   4

in   on   under   next to

5 Choose and write.

~~on~~   next to   under   on   in

1 The children are ____on____ the climbing frame.
2 The cats are _____ the tree house.
3 The ball is _____ the slide.
4 The dog is _____ the climbing frame.
5 The girl is _____ the swing.

6 Play the game.

ball   children   girl   cats   dog

Where's the ball?

It's under the tree.

No, it's under the slide.

My town.

1 Look at the photos. What can you see? Point and say.

2 Listen and read. Then look at the photos and write Z (Zoe) or J (Jake). •))

a Z
b ☐
c ☐
d ☐
e ☐
f ☐

1
My town is big. There are lots of shops and there are lots of cars, too. There's a big park and there are lots of trees. There's a zoo with lots of animals. There's a swimming pool but there isn't a river.
Zoe

2
My town is small. There aren't lots of cars but there are lots of bikes. There's a school and there's a playground next to the school. There isn't a swimming pool in my town but there's a river.
Jake

3 Read again and write yes or no.

Zoe
1 There are lots of bikes. __no__
2 There's a park. _____
3 There's a river. _____

Jake
4 There are lots of cars. _____
5 There's a playground. _____
6 There's a swimming pool. _____

4 Listen and match. •))

1 (Kate and Peter)   **2** (Jane and Anna)   **3** (Bill and May)   **4** (Simon and Matt)

5 Look at 4 and write.

1	Where are Kate and Peter?	They're in the ___playground___ .
2	Where are Simon and Matt?	They're in the _____ .
3	Where are Bill and May?	They're at the _____ .
4	Where are Jane and Anna?	They're at the _____ .

6 Make cards. Then act out. 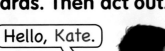 page 107

Hello, Kate.

I'm bored.

Good idea! Come on!

Hello, Peter. What's the matter?

I know, let's go to the playground.

1   **Listen, point and say.** 🔊

ride   swim   climb   sing   jump   high   play the guitar

2   **Listen and read.** 🔊

1 Wow! Look at Karla. She can jump very high!

2 Be careful, Tag!   He can ride his bike very fast.

3 Patty can swim. She's fantastic!

4 Chatter can climb trees!   Look at me. I can sing. I can play the guitar, listen!

No, you can't! That's terrible.

It's OK, Chatter.

3   **Read again. Find and circle the name.**

1 I can jump high. Sally / (Karla)

2 I can swim. Patty / Karla

3 I can ride my bike fast. Tag / Trumpet

4 I can climb trees. Trumpet / Chatter

66

4 Let's learn! Listen and say. •))

Look at Patty.
She can swim.

Look at Chatter.
He can't play the guitar.

5 Choose and write.

sing   climb a tree   ride a bike   jump very high

1

2

3

4

1 _He can't ride a bike._   3 _____

2 _____   4 _____

6 Look at 5. Point and say.

 He can't ride a bike.   Number 1.

7 Sing along with the band! •))

Look, look, look at me.
I can climb a tree.
I can read and I can write.
I can ride a bike.
Look, look, look at me.
I can swim in the sea.
I can jump up very high.
I can touch the sky.
Look, look, look at me.
I can count to three.
I can clap and turn around.
I can touch the ground.

Can you skip?

1 Listen, point and say. •))

rollerblade

fly

skip

do a handstand

walk

run

carry

2 Listen and read. •))

1 Come and play, Trumpet. Can you rollerblade?

No, I can't.

2 Can you fly a kite?

No, I can't. I can't skip. I can't do a handstand.

3 They can do lots of things. I can't.

Yes, you can. You can walk and run.

4 You can carry everyone. We can't carry you!

3 **Read again and write** Chatter, Patty, Tag **or** Trumpet.

1 _____Chatter_____ can rollerblade.
2 _____ can fly a kite.

3 _____ can carry everyone.
4 _____ can do a handstand.

4 Let's learn! Listen and say. •))

Can he skip? Yes, he can.

Can they fly? No, they can't.

5 Listen and tick or cross. •))

✔ = can   ✗ = can't

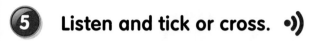

✔ □ □ □ □

6 Look at 5. Write Yes, she can or No, she can't.

1 Can Chloe do a handstand? _Yes, she can._   3 Can she skip? _____

2 Can she play the guitar? _____   4 Can she rollerblade? _____

7 Look and play the game.

Can they climb trees?

Yes, they can.

Can they run?

No, they can't.

Snakes.

	run	climb trees	fly	jump
🐻🐻	✔	✔	✗	✔
🐍	✗	✔	✗	✗
🐰🐰	✔	✗	✗	✔
🦅🦅	✗	✗	✔	✗

Where's my mobile phone?

1 Listen, point and say. •))

2 Listen and read. •))

3 Read again and circle.

1 The pens are on / under the desk.
2 The mobile phone is / isn't in the cupboard.
3 There are lots of books in / on the bookcase.
4 Kelly / Fred has got the phone.
5 It's under / in his bed.

mobile phone
 cupboard
 computer
 bookcase
 table
 bed

④ Choose and write.

cupboard   bed   ~~mobile phone~~   computer   table

Mum can't find her (1) __mobile phone__ . It isn't in the (2) _____ .
It isn't under the (3) _____ . It isn't on the (4) _____ .
Fred's got the phone! It's in his (5) _____ !

⑤ Listen again. Then act out. •))

71

Science

How many senses have we got?

1 **Listen, point and read.** •))

We see with our eyes. We can see colours and pictures. You can see lots of colours in this picture – purple, yellow, white, green, pink and blue!

a 1

b

We hear with our ears. We can hear songs and music. You can listen to music on a mobile phone.

c

d

e

We smell with our noses. We can smell flowers and plants.

We taste with our mouths. We can taste chicken and pasta and ice cream. Ice cream is good!

We touch things with our hands. We can touch our pets. This is my cat.

2 **Listen and number.** •))

3 **Read again and write.**

1 We ___see___ with our eyes.
2 We _____ with our ears.
3 We _____ with our noses.

4 We _____ with our mouths.
5 We _____ with our hands.

4 Look and tick or cross.

1 Things we can see 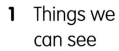 ✓  ☐  ☐ ☐

2 Things we can hear ☐ ☐ ☐  ☐

3 Things we can smell ☐ ☐ ☐ ☐

4 Things we can taste ☐  ☐ ☐  ☐

5 Things we can touch ☐ ☐  ☐ ☐

5 Look at 4. Ask and answer.

Can you see colours? Yes.

Can you see music? No.

6 Your project! Write about your senses. Draw or find pictures.

In my classroom, I can see desks and chairs. I can see pupils, too.

In the canteen, I can smell chicken and pasta.

In the garden, I can smell flowers.

Review 4

1 Choose and write.

desk   slide   trees   cupboard   flowers   swimming pool   swing
bed   school   swans   climbing frame   ~~park~~

1 In our town, there's a _____park_____ , a _____
   and a _____ .

2 In the park there are _____ , _____
   and _____ .

3 In the playground, there's a _____ , a _____
   and a _____ .

4 In my bedroom, there's a _____ , a _____
   and a _____ .

2 Listen and tick or cross. Then play. •))

	Toby	May	Mark	Lucy
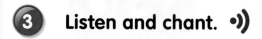	✔			

In my town, there's a park.

Are you Mark?

No. There's a park and a swimming pool.

You're Toby!

3 Listen and chant. •))

There's a snake on the cake.

④ **Play the game.**

Start 1

The climbing frame is .... the trees. 2

Can Bill jump very high? 3

4

The boy is .... the climbing frame. 5

Well done! 20

6

The mobile phone is .... the bag. 19

The kite is .... the table. 7

18

Can the dog rollerblade? 8

Can the girls do a handstand? 17

Can the cat climb the tree? 9

16

10

The bike is .... the slide. 15

Can Kim skip? 14

13

The ducks are .... the treehouse. 12

The bus is .... the park. 11

1 Listen, point and say. •))

 breakfast

 bread

 honey

 milk

 egg

 orange

 hungry

2 Listen and read. •))

1 It's time for breakfast.

Hooray! Thank you, Sally. I like breakfast.

2 I'm hungry! I like bread and honey and milk.

3 I like apples and oranges. I don't like eggs.

You like breakfast and they like breakfast. Trumpet, you're very naughty. Here you are.

4 Where's our breakfast?

Trumpet! We like breakfast, too!

3 Read again and circle.

1 Trumpet is sad / hungry.
2 There's bread / cake for breakfast.

3 There are crisps / eggs for breakfast.
4 Trumpet is very naughty / good.

4 Let's learn! Listen and say. •))

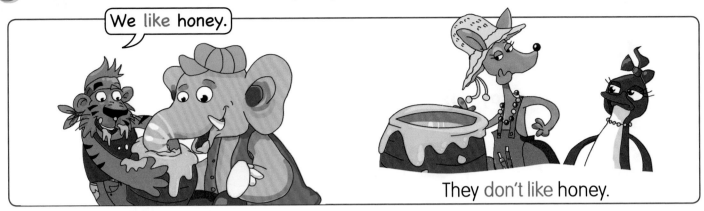

We like honey.

They don't like honey.

5 Listen and stick. Then write like or don't like. •))

1 I _____like_____ apples and eggs. I _____ bread.
2 My brothers _____ bread.
3 Yes, we _____ bread and honey.
4 They _____ milk.

6 Sing along with the band! •))

I like milk and I like bread.
I like honey and I like eggs.
I like apples and oranges too.
I like breakfast.
How about you?

I like breakfast in the morning.
I like breakfast in the morning.
I like breakfast in the morning.
I like breakfast.
How about you?

Patty likes fish.

1 Listen, point and say. •))

 lunch

 spaghetti

 soup

 chicken

 potatoes

 fish

2 Listen and read. •))

1 It's time for lunch.

Do you want spaghetti, Karla?

Yes, please. I like spaghetti.

2 Do you want soup, Patty?

No, thank you. I don't like soup.

3 Do you like chicken, Patty? Do you like potatoes?

No, I don't!

4 Patty doesn't like salad. She likes fish.

5 Thank you, Trumpet. I love fish.

3 Read again and circle.

1 It's time for breakfast.   yes / no
2 Tag has got pizza.   yes / no

3 Sally has got soup.   yes / no
4 Patty has got fish.   yes / no

4 Let's learn! Listen and say. •))

Tag likes chicken.
He doesn't like oranges.

5 Look and write likes or doesn't like.

1 Tom _____likes_____ chicken.
2 He _____ soup.
3 He _____ potatoes.

4 He _____ pizza.
5 He _____ fish.
6 He _____ oranges.

6 Draw. Then ask and answer.

	 soup bowl	fish	pizza	chicken
Me	😊	😊	😊	😊
My friend	😊	😊	😊	😊

Do you like soup?
Do you like fish?

Yes, I do.
No, I don't.

7 Tell the class.

Sarah likes soup. She doesn't like fish.

What's on the menu?

9c

1 Look at the menu. Find the words and say.

2 Listen and read. What do they like? Write D (Daisy) or A (Adam). •))

Your choice of kids' meals

MAIN COURSES

SOUP D
and bread

SANDWICHES
cheese and tomato
or chicken and tomato

PIZZA
and salad

SPAGHETTI A
and tomato or
cheese sauce

CHICKEN
and spaghetti

BURGER
and mashed potato

2 SAUSAGES
and mashed potato

FISH AND CHIPS

SAUSAGES AND EGG

DESSERTS

ICE CREAM
JELLY
FRUIT
apple, orange
or banana

DRINKS

APPLE JUICE
ORANGE JUICE
WATER

Daisy

I'm hungry. What's on the menu? I like soup. I like pizza and salad, too. I don't like burgers or sausages. For dessert, I like bananas and oranges but I don't like apples. I like orange juice. What about you, Adam?

Adam

I love spaghetti and tomato sauce. I like cheese and tomato sandwiches, too. I don't like chicken or fish and chips. For dessert, I love ice cream but I don't like jelly. I like apple juice and orange juice but I don't like water.

3 Read again and say.

Daisy doesn't like ...   Adam doesn't like ...

4 Listen and match. •))

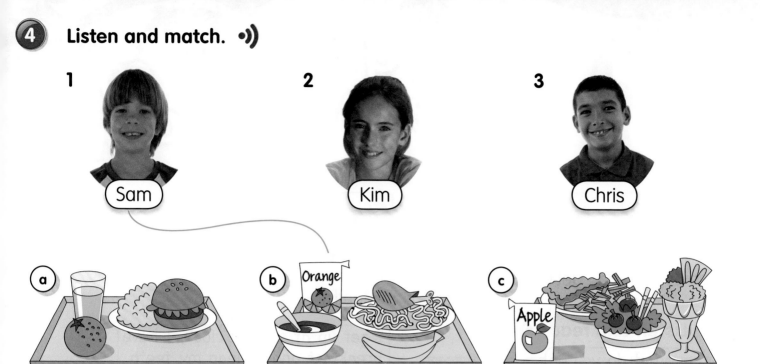

1 Sam

2 Kim

3 Chris

a

b Orange

c Apple

5 Look at 4 and write.

1 Sam wants _____soup_____ and _____,
a _____ and _____ .
2 Kim wants _____ and _____,
_____ and _____ .
3 Chris wants a _____ and _____,
an _____ and _____ .

6 Make cards. Then act out. page 109

Hello. Can I have pizza, please?

Yes, of course. Do you want a dessert?

Yes, can I have ice cream, please?

Anything else?

Yes. Orange juice, please.

Pizza, ice cream and orange juice.

He gets up at seven o'clock.

1 Listen, point and say. •))

seven o'clock

get up

have breakfast

clean my teeth

go to school

2 Listen and read. •))

1 What do you do every day, Rob?

2 I get up at seven o'clock, I have breakfast and I clean my teeth. I go to school at eight o'clock.

3 He gets up at seven o'clock, he has breakfast and he cleans his teeth. He goes to school at eight o'clock every day.

Oh!

4 What's the time?
It's eight o'clock.
Let's go to his school!

Yes!

3 Read again and number in order.

        [1]

a   b   c   d

4 Let's learn! Listen and say. •))

He cleans his teeth every day.
She gets up at seven o'clock every day.
It drinks milk every day.

5 Look, write and circle.

| 1 | 2 | 3 | 4 |

1 _____She gets up_____ at five o'clock / (seven o'clock).
2 _____ at seven o'clock / eight o'clock.
3 _____ at four o'clock / six o'clock.
4 _____ at eight o'clock / nine o'clock.

6 Look at 5. What about you?

I get up at six o'clock every day. I go to ...

7 Sing along with the band! •))

Every day at three o'clock,
I come to the zoo.
I see my friends and we all play,
In my favourite zoo.

Chatter and Trumpet,
Karla and Tag,
Patty and Sally too.
They love me and I love them.
We all love our zoo.

Every day at three o'clock,
He goes to the zoo.
He sees his friends and they all play,
In his favourite zoo.

Chatter and Trumpet,
Karla and Tag,
Patty and Sally too.
They love him
And he loves them.
They all love,
We all love our zoo!

1 Listen, point and say. •))

 Monday
 Tuesday
 Wednesday
 Thursday
 Friday
 Saturday
 Sunday

2 Listen and read. •))

3 Read again and circle.

1 Mr Light is a teacher. yes / no
2 Rob goes to school every day. yes / no
3 Rob goes to the zoo every day. yes / no
4 The children love the zoo. yes / no

4 Let's learn! Listen and say. •))

Does he go to school every day? No, he doesn't.
Does he play basketball every day? Yes, he does.

5 Listen and circle. Then answer. •))

Monday

Thursday

Tuesday

Friday

Wednesday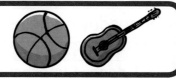

1 Does Rob ride his bike on Monday?   Yes, he does.
2 Does Rob swim on Tuesday?   _____
3 Does Rob play the guitar on Wednesday?   _____
4 Does Rob play basketball on Thursday?   _____
5 Does Rob go to the park on Friday?   _____

6 Play the game.

Look at me. What day is it?

Is it Friday?

Yes, it is!

Superboy!

Superboy helps people every day of the week.

I'm Superboy! I am very strong. I can fly!

On Monday he helps old people.

Thank you, Superboy!

It's my pleasure.

On Tuesday he helps children.

Thank you, Superboy!

Have a good day, children!

On Wednesday he helps police officers.

Well done, Superboy!

Don't mention it!

1 Listen, point and say. •))

2 Listen and read. •))

3 Read again and circle.

1 Does Superboy help old people on Monday? Yes, he does. / No, he doesn't.

2 Does he help police officers on Tuesday? Yes, he does. / No, he doesn't.

3 Does he help children on Wednesday? Yes, he does. / No, he doesn't.

4 Does he help firefighters on Thursday? Yes, he does. / No, he doesn't.

5 Does he do his homework every day of the week? Yes, he does. / No, he doesn't.

people police officer firefighter help visit do my homework

On Thursday he helps firefighters.

On Friday he helps animals.

On Saturday he visits his grandma and grandpa.

But on Sunday he does his homework. Help Superboy with his homework!

4 **Choose and write.**

visits   police officers   helps   ~~people~~   firefighters   homework   animals

Superboy helps (1) _____people_____ every day. On Monday he
(2) _____ old people. On Tuesday he helps children. On Wednesday
he helps (3) _____ and on Thursday he helps (4) _____ .
On Friday he helps (5) _____ . On Saturday he (6) _____
his grandma and grandpa. On Sunday he does his (7) _____ .

5 **Listen again. Then act out.** •))

87

Social Science

How can you stay healthy?

1 Listen, point and read. •))

Healthy Harry

This is Harry. He's eight. Harry is very healthy.

Sleep well. ☐

Harry goes to bed at 8 o'clock. He gets up at 7 o'clock. He sleeps well! Lots of sleep helps him work well at school.

Clean your teeth. ☐

Harry cleans his teeth every morning and night. His teeth are white and strong.

Wash your hands. ☐

Harry washes his hands before meals and after he goes to the toilet.

Eat lots of fruit. ☐1

Harry eats fruit every day. He likes oranges and apples. He doesn't eat sweets or chips. They aren't healthy.

Exercise every day. ☐

Harry doesn't watch TV or play computer games. After school, he plays with his friends. They play games and sports.

2 Listen and number. •))

3 Draw 😊 or 😕 .

	Healthy	Not healthy
1 Wash your hands before meals.	😊	😕
2 Eat sweets every day.	😕	😕
3 Clean your teeth every morning and night.	😕	😕
4 Play computer games after school.	😕	😕
5 Sleep well.	😕	😕

4 Are you healthy? Ask and answer. Then draw 😊 or 😕 .

Me	😕	😕	😕	😕
My friend	😕	😕	😕	😕

Do you clean your teeth every morning and night? Yes, I do.

Do you wash your hands before meals?

5 **Your project!** Write about your life. Draw or find pictures.

I eat fruit every day.

I play sports.

I don't watch TV.

I don't eat sweets every day.

Review 5

1 **Listen and circle the food they like.** •))

1 (spaghetti) tomatoes
milk   apples

2 fish   bread
sausages   soup

3 chicken   potatoes
oranges   cheese

4 eggs   bananas
honey   salad

2 **Ask and answer about you.**

Do you like spaghetti?   Yes, I do.

3 **Ask and answer. Then tell the class.**

1 Do you get up at six o'clock? yes / no
2 Do you have eggs for breakfast? yes / no
3 Do you play basketball every day? yes / no
4 Do you go to the park after school? yes / no
5 Do you visit your grandma and grandpa on Sunday? yes / no

Monica doesn't get up at six o'clock.
She gets up at seven o'clock.

4 **Listen and chant.** •))

A slide, a bike and five white kites.

11a I'm playing a game.

1 **Listen, point and say.** •))

play

read

sleep

hide

come

water pistol

2 **Listen and read.** •))

1
Sally, I'm doing my homework! I'm reading.

I'm writing.

Very good!

2
Look at Chatter. He's sleeping.

3
Ssh!

Oh, you're hiding!

Yes! I'm playing a game.

4
Tag has got a big water pistol! Run! He's coming!

3 **Look at 2 and circle.**

1 Patty has got a phone / pencil.

2 Trumpet has got a book / pen.

3 Tag has got homework / a water pistol.

4 The water pistol is small / big.

4 Let's learn! Listen and say. •))

Who is it?
He's doing his homework.
She's writing.
He's playing a game.

> I'm hiding.

5 Listen and stick. Then write. •))

1 I'm ___reading___ .   **2** He's _____ .   **3** She's _____ .

6 Look and say.

> She's doing her homework.
> Number 4.

 **1**
 **4**
 **2**
 **5**
 **3**
 6

7 Sing along with the band! •))

I'm playing with my friends.
I'm playing with my friends.
Hey ho, away we go.
I'm playing with my friends.

She's hiding from her friends.
She's hiding from her friends.
Hey ho, away we go.
She's hiding from her friends.

They're having a shower.

1 Listen, point and say. 🔊

 wet

 dry

 trousers

 shoes

 dress

 sweater

 have a shower

2 Listen and read. 🔊

3 Read again and circle.

1 Sally is wearing a skirt. yes / no
2 Patty is wearing a T-shirt. yes / no
3 Chatter is playing in the river. yes / no
4 Tag is having a shower. yes / no

94

4 Let's learn! Listen and say. •))

5 Listen and number. Then circle and write. •))

1 (We're) / They're wearing ___green trousers___ .
2 We're / They're wearing _____ .
3 We're / They're wearing _____ .
4 We're / They're wearing _____ .

6 Look at 5 and say.

They're wearing pink dresses.

Number 4.

7 Play the game. Who is it?

He's wearing a purple sweater.

No, it isn't. He's wearing black trousers and black shoes.

Yes!

Is it Peter?

It's Alex.

Me and my friends.

1 **Look at the pictures. What can you see? Point and say.**

2 **Look and read. Then write a or b.**

1 There are three children. ___a___
2 The girl is hiding. _____
3 There's a robot under the chair. _____
4 The cat is sleeping. _____

5 The girl is reading. _____
6 The boy has got a computer game. _____
7 There's a computer on the desk. _____
8 The boys are playing a game. _____

3 **Look at 2 and write yes or no.**

Picture (a)

1 The girl is wearing a blue dress.
___yes___
2 The boys are wearing green sweaters.
_____
3 The girl is wearing a yellow T-shirt.
_____

Picture (b)

4 The girls are wearing blue skirts.
_____
5 The boy is wearing red trousers.
_____
6 The doll is wearing a purple skirt.
_____

4 **Listen and match.** •))

Mary

Helen

Daniel

Rosa

Nick

Tom

5 **Look at 4 and write the names.**

1 _____Mary_____ is wearing her new watch.
2 _____ and _____ are flying kites.
3 _____ has got short black hair.
4 _____ and _____ are wearing red T-shirts.
5 _____ is hiding.
6 _____ is doing a handstand.

6 **Look at 4 and say.**

She's wearing a white dress.

Right. Your turn.

It's Daniel.

It's Mary.

He's got a red kite.

They aren't swimming.

1 Listen, point and say. •))

 basketball
 volleyball
 football
 tennis
 idea
 tired

2 Listen and read. •))

Tag is playing basketball. I'm not playing basketball.

Karla and Trumpet are playing volleyball. I'm not playing volleyball.

I'm not playing football. I'm not playing tennis.

I've got a good idea!

You're swimming, Patty! They aren't swimming!

I'm tired.

3 Look at 2. Find and write the name.

1 He's playing basketball. ___Tag___   3 He's playing football. _____
2 They're playing volleyball. _____   4 She's swimming. _____

4 Let's learn! Listen and say. •))

I'm not playing football.

He isn't playing football.

We aren't playing tennis.

They aren't swimming.

5 Look and write is/isn't or are/aren't.

a
1 The dog ___is___ sleeping.
2 The girls _____ playing tennis.
3 The boys _____ playing basketball.
4 The baby _____ walking.
5 The cat _____ hiding.

b
1 The dog ___isn't___ sleeping.
2 The girls _____ playing tennis.
3 The boys _____ playing basketball.
4 The baby _____ walking.
5 The cat _____ hiding.

6 Sing along with the band! •))

I'm not playing basketball.
I'm not playing volleyball.
I'm not playing football.
I'm not playing tennis.

I'm swimming in the sea today.
I'm splashing in the sea today.
Splish and splash,
Splish and splash,
I'm swimming in the sea today.

1 Listen, point and say. •))

noise   dream   drink   roar   snore   upstairs

2 Listen and sing. •))

① Are they sleeping? Are they dreaming?
Where are the animals?
What are they doing?
Are they reading? Are they writing?
What is that terrible noise?

Are you eating? Are you drinking?
Where are you, animals?
What are you doing?
Are you playing? Are you hiding?
What is that terrible noise?

② Hide all the toys! Eat all the cake!
Jump into bed! Sally is coming upstairs!

③ We're not playing.
We're not eating.
Look at us, Sally,
We're very good animals.
Tag's not roaring.
Trumpet's snoring.
That is the terrible noise!

3 Let's learn! Listen and say. •))

Are you sleeping, Tag?

No, I'm not.

Is Tag sleeping?
No, he isn't.
Are the animals sleeping?
No, they aren't.
Are they eating?
Yes, they are.

4 Listen and circle. Then answer. •))

 yes / (no)

 yes / no

 yes / no

 yes / no

 yes / no

 yes / no

1 Is Bella doing her homework?   _No, she isn't._
2 Is she having a shower?   _____
3 Is George reading?   _____
4 Is he writing?   _____
5 Is Dad sleeping?   _____
6 Are Bella, George and Dad playing on the computer?   _____

5 Make cards. Then play the game.

 page 111

Are you having a shower?

No, I'm not. Guess again.

Jane can see a big house. It's got lots of doors and windows. She can hear a noise.

① Hey, ho, hi, humming. I'm a giant. I am coming!

Jane is in the living room. She's hiding under a table. She can hear the giant.

② Micky, mocky, mucky, mig! I'm a giant. I am big.

Jane is in the bathroom now. She's hiding in the shower. She can hear the giant.

③ Flippy, floppy, flappy, flong! I'm a giant. I am strong.

Jane is in the kitchen. She's hiding in the cupboard. She can hear the giant.

④ Wiz, woz, woodle, weet! I'm a giant. I've got big feet.

1 Listen, point and say. •))   **2** Listen and read. •))

3 Look, choose and write.

kitchen   living room   ~~bedroom~~   bathroom

1 Jane is hiding in the bed here.   _bedroom_
2 Jane is hiding in the cupboard here. _____
3 Jane is hiding under the table here. _____
4 Jane is hiding in the shower here.   _____

giant living room bathroom kitchen bedroom scared

Jane is in the bedroom now. She's hiding in the bed. She can hear the giant.

5 Bing, bang, bong, begs! I'm a giant. I've got long legs.

6 He's got a big head, long arms and big feet!

I can hear a girl!

Jane has got a good idea. She's standing on the bed.

7 Apples, jelly, cakes and toast! Look at me. I'm a ghost!

8 The giant is scared.

Goodnight, giant. Sweet dreams!

4 **Choose and write.**

scared   arms   giant   ~~hear~~   ghost   strong

Jane can see a big house. She can (1) _____hear_____ a noise. There's a
(2) _____ in the house. He's coming for Jane. She's hiding. The giant is
(3) _____. He's got a big head, long (4) _____ and big feet. Jane
has got a good idea. She says, 'Look at me. I'm a (5) _____!' The giant is
(6) _____!

5 **Listen again. Then act out.** •))

 103

Social Science

What kind of home do you live in?

1 Listen, point and read. •))

Hi! I'm Amaya. I'm from Japan. My home is a small flat in a big city. We live and eat in one room. There are two bedrooms and a small bathroom. The city is noisy but it's quiet in my home.

My name is Harvey. I'm from America. I live in a mobile home. It's in a big park. It's got three bedrooms, a bathroom, a living room and a big kitchen. We've got a pretty garden with lots of flowers.

1

I'm Ajay and I live in India. My home is a houseboat. It's very long. It's got a living room, a small kitchen, a bathroom and two bedrooms. My home is on a river. I love it!

Hello. I'm Frida. I live in Sweden. My home is a wooden house. It's in the country. There's a living room, a kitchen and three bedrooms. There are two bathrooms. There are lots of trees next to my home. It's beautiful!

2 Listen and number. •))

3 Read again and write.

1 Ajay lives in _____India_____. His home is a _____.
2 Harvey lives in _____. His home is a _____.
3 Frida lives in _____. Her home is a _____.
4 Amaya lives in _____. Her home is a _____.

4 **Read again and match.**

1 There are three bedrooms. There are two bathrooms.   **a** mobile home
2 There are two bedrooms and a small kitchen.   **b** houseboat
3 There are three bedrooms. There's a big kitchen.   **c** flat
4 There are two bedrooms and a small bathroom.   **d** wooden house

5 **Read and answer. Who is it?**

1
> His home is on a river. It's very long. It's ____Ajay____ .

3
> She lives in the country. There are lots of trees next to her home. It's _____ .

2
> She lives in a city. She lives and eats in one room. It's _____ .

4
> His home is in a park. It's got a garden. It's _____ .

6 **Your project!** Compare your homes. Write and draw or find pictures.

I'm from Poland.
My home is a flat. It's in the country.
There are three bedrooms and a big living room.

Amaya is from Japan.
Her home is a flat, too.
It's in a city.
There are two bedrooms and a small bathroom.

Review 6

1 **Circle the odd one out. Then write.**

1 basketball volleyball (bedroom) football _____bedroom_____
2 giant kitchen living room bathroom _____
3 eat dream drink T-shirt _____
4 trousers shower sweater skirt _____

2 **Listen and circle. Then answer.** •))

The giant is in the (kitchen) / bedroom. He's playing / doing his homework. His mum is snoring / writing. His dad is playing football / tennis in the living room / kitchen. His brother and sister are having a shower / hiding in the shower.

1 Is the giant in the kitchen? _____Yes, he is._____
2 Is the giant doing his homework? _____
3 Is his mum writing? _____
4 Is his dad playing tennis? _____
5 Are his brother and sister having a shower? _____

3 **Answer about you.**

1 Are you writing in your book? _____
2 Are you standing up? _____
3 Are you wearing trousers? _____
4 What are you doing? _____

4 **Listen and chant.** •))

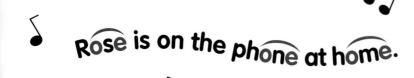

Rose is on the phone at home.

5 Play the game.

Start 1	What's Ella wearing? 2	3	What are the boys playing? 4	5
Well done! 20				6
Are the monkeys eating? 19				What are the tigers doing? 7
18				8
What is the lion doing? 17				Is Peter reading a book? 9
16		WILDLIFE PARK		10
Is the baby sleeping? 15	14	What's Toby wearing? 13	12	Are the girls scared? 11

Peter

Toby

Ella

The YAZoo

Sally: Hello! I'm Sally and I'm the keeper in our zoo!

All sing: My name's Trumpet, how are you?

Child 1: There's a monkey, a tiger, a kangaroo, a penguin and an elephant in the zoo.

All sing: There are lots of animals in our zoo. (Unit 7a)

Trumpet: I'm Trumpet. I'm an elephant. I like school.

Karla: I'm Karla. I'm a kangaroo. At school we read and write and play.

Child 2: Do you go to school every day?

Trumpet: No. We go to school on Monday, Tuesday, Wednesday, Thursday and Friday.

Child 1: Are you happy today?

All: Yes, we are!

All sing: Stand up and say. (Unit 4a)

Chatter:	My name is Chatter. I'm a monkey. I can climb trees!
Patty:	I'm Patty. I'm a penguin. I can swim in the sea.
Tag:	My name is Tag. I'm a tiger. I can play basketball.
All sing:	Look, look, look at me. (Unit 8a)
Child 2:	I'm hungry! Have we got any apples and oranges? I like apples and oranges!
All sing:	I like milk and I like bread. (Unit 9a)
Child 1:	Sally, are the animals in the zoo good?
Sally:	Yes, they are!
Children 1 & 2:	We love the animals in the zoo!
All sing:	Every day at three o'clock. (Unit 10a)
Sally:	We love our families and friends! We love you!
All sing:	Clap and dance and sing with me. (Unit 3a)
All:	Goodbye!

World Animal Day

1 **Listen, point and say.** •))

food

water

home

exercise

2 **Listen and read.** •))

Today is World Animal Day. On World Animal Day we think about animals and pets. We give our pets lots of things.

We give our pets a home.

We give our pets food and water.

We give our pets exercise.

We give our pets lots of love, too.

3 Look and match.

a | b | c | d | e

1 Here's your new home. __b__
2 This is your food. _____
3 That's your water. _____

4 This is your exercise ball. _____
5 He's a happy pet! _____

4 Listen and sing.

Let's play with our pets,
Play with our pets today.
Let's play with our pets today,
Today and every day.

Let's love our pets,
Love our pets today.
Let's love our pets today,
Today and every day.

5 Make an animal mask. Then ask and answer.

Is your pet a cat?

No, it isn't.

Is it a rabbit?

Yes, it is.

International Children's Day

1 **Listen, point and say.** •))

world

picnic

art

swap

2 **Listen, read and match.** •))

> People celebrate International Children's Day around the world.

a

b

c

d

1 At our school we have a picnic. ___c___

2 We have an art day. _____

3 We swap toys. _____

4 We have a show. _____

3 **Listen and sing.** •))

We're friends, friends,
Friends forever.
We learn together,
Play together,
Have fun together.
We're friends together,
Forever.

4 **Make a card.**